THEN & NOW®

GROSSE POINTE

Opposite: Please see page 12.

THEN & NOW®

GROSSE POINTE

Ann Marie Aliotta and Suzy Berschback

Library of Congress control number: 2007924629

Published by Arcadia Publishing
Charleston, South Carolina

Printed in the United States of America

Then and Now is a registered trademark and is used under license from
Salamander Books Limited

For all general information contact Arcadia Publishing at:
Telephone 843-853-2070
Fax 843-853-0044
E-mail sales@arcadiapublishing.com
For customer service and orders:
Toll-Free 1-888-313-2665

Visit us on the Internet at www.arcadiapublishing.com

This book is dedicated to Suzy Berschback's mother,
Marilyn S. King, who shared her passion for Grosse Pointe history;
and to Ann Marie Aliotta's family—Jerry, Sophia, Joey, and
Francesca—for their support and patience during this project.

On the front cover: Please see page 62. (Historic image courtesy of the Grosse Pointe Historical
Society, contemporary image courtesy of Suzy Berschback.)

On the back cover: SUNDAY DRIVER. Taking a leisurely ride down Lake Shore Road has
been a popular diversion since the road was constructed. This 19th-century horse-and-buggy
driver most assuredly enjoyed the view of Lake St. Clair and the Victorian summer cottages,
boathouses, and lakefront windmills. In front of him can be seen the old McMillan-Newberry
dock. (Courtesy of the Grosse Pointe Historical Society.)

CONTENTS

ACKNOWLEDGMENTS

We would like to thank everyone who called us with information, took time to answer our questions, and gave us photographs for this project. Thank you to Lisa Mower Gandelot, Chip Berschback, and Jerry Aliotta for proofreading. Thank you to the Grosse Pointe Historical Society for their willingness to open the photograph archives for this project.

Thank you to the following people for their time, efforts, and photographic contributions toward this project: Bill and Mary Jo Huntington, John Minnis, John Parthum, Linda Johnson, the Grosse Pointe Woods Historical Commission, J. J. Hile, Amy Silverston, Lauren Miller, the Edsel and Eleanor Ford House, Jay Hunter, Sally Cudlip, Bill Krag, the Country Club of Detroit, Sue Cieslak, Belle Isle Awning Company, the Grosse Pointe Chamber of Commerce, Danielle DeFauw, Mike Mulier, Dave Charvat, Liz Jefferies, Dick Graves, Posterity Gallery, the Great Frame Up, Joan Murphy, Kim North Shine, Mark Wollenweber, Grosse Pointe Questers Chapter 147 and the League of Women Voters, Madeleine Socia, Paula Jarvis, Jean Dodenhoff, Brad Lindberg, Ineke Bruynooghe, Mary Anne Brush, Vickey Bloom, Mason Ferry, Kenneth Schramm, Kathleen Gallagher Kedzierski, Stuart Grigg, John T. Woodhouse Jr., and Lochmoor Ace Harware.

Other sources consulted while writing this book were *Tonnancour: Life in Grosse Pointe and along the Shores of Lake St. Clair*, Vol. 1 and 2, edited by Arthur M. Woodford; *Grosse Pointe 1880–1930* by Madeleine Socia and Suzy Berschback; *AIA Detroit* by Eric J. Hill, FAIA, and John Gallagher; *The Buildings of Detroit* by W. Hawkins Ferry; *Grosse Pointe on Lake Sainte Clair* by Theodore Parsons Hall and Silas Farmer; *Heritage: A Journal of Grosse Pointe Life* magazine; "A Walk Through Time" by the Grosse Pointe Farms Historical Advisory Commission; and the Grosse Pointe Historical Society Web site, www.gphistorical.org.

INTRODUCTION

Stand on any street corner in Grosse Pointe and close your eyes. Let your mind travel back in time and what do you see? A Chippewa Indian hunting game with a bow and arrow; a French habitant cultivating the land on ribbon farms running up to the lake; and a society debutant playing croquet on the lawn of her estate. All of these could have taken place on the same site over the years.

Grosse Pointe is one of the oldest communities in the Midwest with roots dating back to the mid-1600s. People from different backgrounds, cultures, and resources have shared the same little bit of land on the banks of Lake St. Clair. Its history is as varied and vibrant as its many inhabitants.

Take a look at some of the different cultural, civic, and commercial institutions to get a better idea of Grosse Pointe's evolutions. High-quality education, a constant cornerstone of the community, started as a one-room schoolhouse that was built in the 1850s. Today the public school system is one of the finest in the country with high academic standards.

Religious establishments have also grown and evolved with the community's needs and wants. Church buildings have been transformed to accommodate growing membership and changing styles of worship and reflection.

Compact but busy commercial districts have developed over the years and changed with the times and tastes of each generation. Depending on one's age, one might have bought that special outfit at Jacobson's or Coldwater Creek, and afterward, enjoyed a sweet treat at Sanders or Caribou Coffee. Mack Avenue, one of the main thoroughfares in Grosse Pointe, served as a Native American pathway and French settler road before it was paved with asphalt.

By the early 20th century, Grosse Pointe was becoming the fashionable place for successful Detroit businessmen to build their palatial estates. With names like the Moorings and Stonehurst, these residences were designed by nationally known architects, adding to the cachet of the area. Today only a few of these mansions remain; most have been torn down for new subdivisions where many houses occupy the location.

More than just the names on the storefronts and houses on the streets have changed. The change in Grosse Pointe has reflected the changes in America, as the manufacturing industry rose and fell in prominence, and as the middle class grew, putting the dream of owning a house in a comfortable suburb within the reach of more people.

Reconciling growth and progress with preservation and tradition can be difficult, and the Grosse Pointe community has not been immune to its challenges. The financial burden of maintaining some of the structures that embody our history is great, and many of these buildings have been demolished. We hope this book, with its look back at the evolution of buildings and sites in Grosse Pointe, will help celebrate its rich history and preserve it for generations to come. To learn more about Grosse Pointe history, visit www.gphistorical.org.

CHAPTER 1

THERE'S NO PLACE LIKE HOME

DRYBROOK. Truman Handy and Harriet Barnes Newberry built their Georgian estate in 1914 after returning from Washington, D.C. Truman had served as secretary of the navy under Theodore Roosevelt and as a U.S. senator. Great music lovers, the Newberrys had a magnificent music room with a built-in organ adjacent to an outdoor music court. The Detroit Symphony Orchestra once performed there. After the senator died in 1945, his beloved Drybrook was put up for sale for $75,000. Taxes were $10,000. When no buyers could be found, the mansion was razed in 1950, making room for the 24 homes that now stand on Newberry Place.

STONEHURST. Built in 1915 in the early English Renaissance style, Stonehurst was the home of Dr. Joseph B. Schlotman and his wife, Stella, the granddaughter of John Battice Ford who founded the Michigan Alkali Company. Stella's 40-room, 30,000-square-foot estate was next door to her brother Emory's, and down the street from the homes of her two sisters: Clairview (home of Eleanor Ford Torrey) and Fairholme (home of Hettie Ford Speck). After her husband died in 1951, Stella lived there alone until her death 23 years later. The home was demolished and replaced by a subdivision, but the original low stone wall remains. Stories abound that Stella's ghost roams the property to this day.

DR. H.N. TORREY RES. GROSSE PT. SHORES.

CLAIRVIEW. This Palladian mansion was built for Dr. Henry N. Torrey and his wife, Eleanor. Completed in 1913, the residence was designed by English architect John Scott in the Beaux-Arts style of the Vanderbilt's Marble House in Newport, Rhode Island. At the front of the house, balustraded terraces overlooked formal gardens with hedges and fountains. In the back was a lagoon surrounded by woods. The Torreys donated two acres of this property to the Grosse Pointe Woods Presbyterian church for a new building, which is located on what is now Mack Avenue at Torrey Road. The mansion was demolished in 1960, and the property was subdivided.

BUCK-WARDWELL HOUSE. Believed to be the oldest brick house in Grosse Pointe, this house was built around 1849 out of locally made brick by William Buck, a prosperous farmer from England. It was the only early structure on his 210-acre ribbon farm originally known as Private Claim 391. At one point, Henry Ford wanted to buy the house and relocate it in Greenfield Village, but the owner at the time, Harold Wardwell, refused to sell. The home, which still has two of its original pear trees, remains a private residence today. It is located at Jefferson Avenue and Three Mile Drive.

THE SYCAMORES. In 1922, John Dodge's first child, Winifred, married Wesson Seyburn, scion of an old Detroit family. They built a French country chateau, the Sycamores, on East Jefferson Avenue. The home was located near the lake and approached by an allée of sycamore trees. Formal gardens with clipped fruit trees, gravel walks, geometric flower beds, and sculptures captured the flavor of 18th-century France. Winifred lived there until her death in 1980. The house was razed the following year, and the tree-lined drive was replaced by a narrow, paved street, Sycamore Lane, with 18 luxury houses. The fence and gate pillars that marked the former boundaries of the estate still stand at the entrance to the street.

CADIEUX FARMHOUSE. This white clapboard farmhouse was built in the mid-1800s by Isadore Cadieux, son of Michael Cadieux, one of Grosse Pointe's first settlers. It is one of the oldest houses remaining in Grosse Pointe—but it almost was not so. In 1991, the home was due to fall victim to the wrecking ball when a concerned citizen led a grassroots effort to save it. After a careful restoration, including rebuilding the basement and foundation (the original floors, windows, stairway, and exterior siding remain), the house was put on the market. It was purchased by a local businessman who lives there today (above), much to the delight of the Cadieux descendants and local preservationists.

PARENT STORE. Built in the late 1800s, the A. C. Parent store on Rivard Boulevard between Maumee Street and East Jefferson Avenue sold groceries and dry goods. The building was owned by Parent grocers and their descendants until 1979. Today a wonderful example of adaptive reuse, the building is a four-unit condominium.

ROSE TERRACE. Perhaps the most opulent of the Grosse Pointe mansions was Rose Terrace II, built by Anna Dodge, widow of automobile entrepreneur Horace Dodge, and her second husband, the former actor Hugh Dillman. Sitting on nearly nine acres on Lake St. Clair, the home boasted 42 rooms and 20 baths and cost $4 million to build in 1934. It was filled with art and artifacts from the imperial palaces of Russia, courts of France, and country estates of England. Following Anna's death in 1970, the magnificent structure stood empty until 1976 when it was razed to make way for a subdivision.

THE POPLARS. In the late 1800s, Grosse Pointe was becoming an exclusive summer colony for the newly rich of Detroit. William A. McGraw, a successful real estate developer and son of profitable businessman A. C. McGraw, built this pretty Queen Anne cottage on Lake Shore Road in 1884 (below). It was named the Poplars because of the Lombardy poplar trees on the property's 10 acres, which included a little park that ran down to the lake. In his book *Grosse Pointe on Lake Sainte Claire*, Silas Farmer wrote, "The interior . . . is a model of convenience, and its general finish and tasteful appointments are admired by all." The Poplars is a private residence today, though altered by a 1920s Robert O. Derrick facade and addition (above).

THE MOORINGS. This home was built in 1910 for Russell A. Alger Jr., son of Gen. Russell A. Alger, a celebrated Civil War leader, Michigan governor, and lumber baron. Alger Jr., who helped found the Packard Motor Car Company, commissioned New York architect Charles A. Platt to design the Italianate mansion with extensive gardens on the bluffs overlooking Lake St. Clair. Following Alger's death, the home was a branch of the Detroit Institute of Arts from 1936 to 1948. In 1949, the family donated it to the Grosse Pointe War Memorial Association in honor of World War II veterans. Today it is a community cultural center hosting more than 2,000 events annually.

INTERURBAN RAILWAY ON GROSSE POINTE BOULEVARD. The East Detroit and Grosse Pointe Railway opened in May 1888, bringing travelers from Detroit to Grosse Pointe. It ran along Jefferson Avenue to Fisher Road. Lake Shore Road residents were worried that the tracks would extend along the shoreline, upsetting their view. In 1891, Grosse Pointe Boulevard was developed and opened as a back road for the railway. The tracks ran up Fisher Road to Grosse Pointe Boulevard, on to old Weir Lane (see the wall at the north end of Kercheval Avenue) and back down to Lake Shore Road, where it picked up again and ran all the way to Mount Clemens and eventually Port Huron.

BEVERLY ROAD SUBDIVISION GATE.
Albert Kahn designed these graceful limestone and wrought iron gates that front the Beverly Road subdivision. Established around 1910 by Henry Joy, it was one of the first prestigious residential developments in Grosse Pointe. Designed by many prominent residential architects of the day, including Robert O. Derrick, Raymond Carey, and Marcus Burrowes, 22 houses were built. They all remain today, and the block, which is on the National Register of Historic Districts, is very much a modern family neighborhood. On any given day, one can see kids playing football on the front lawns, shooting hoops in the backyard, and riding bikes and scooters on the enclosed street.

THERE'S NO PLACE LIKE HOME

INTERURBAN WORKERS ON LAKESHORE.
Workers lay tracks along Lake Shore Road north of Provencal Road for the Jefferson Avenue Railway in the late 1890s. This line completed an interurban system that ran all the way from Detroit to Mount Clemens, and eventually Port Huron, through Grosse Pointe and St. Clair Shores. It made Detroit accessible to those who lived near the rail line and brought Detroiters out to Grosse Pointe and beyond for summer excursions. The lines were dismantled in the 1920s, made obsolete by the automobile.

SHORE ROAD. Today's Sunday drivers, in-line skaters, bikers, and joggers enjoy a scenic trip along Lake Shore Road enhanced by flowers and shrubs planted by ongoing beautification projects. They scarcely could imagine that this four-lane divided boulevard was developed from a nine-mile plank road known as the River Road or Grosse Pointe Road, built in 1851. In 1930 and 1931, a Wayne County project filled in the land along the shore to expand the road using dirt taken from the excavations of the new skyscrapers in downtown Detroit.

Grosse Pointe Road, Detroit, Mich.

THERE'S NO PLACE LIKE HOME

KERBY FARMHOUSE. The Kerby family arrived in the Pointes in the late 18th century and became prosperous farmers, fishery owners, and, in the case of young George Kerby, the proprietor of a confectionary store. Rufus M. Kerby, a successful farmer, inherited this house and surrounding property from his grandfather John, who got it from his in-laws. It was built around 1850 on today's Kerby Road and is still a private residence. The home has new brick facing and is missing the original two chimneys.

CHARLES BACKMAN GROCERY STORE. Around 1900, the area near Moross Road and Kercheval Avenue was a little shopping center that included a plumbing shop, valet service, and the Charles Backman grocery store. Locals would stop in for everything from produce to penny candy and even children's shoes. If they wanted, they could have their goods delivered by horse and wagon, which were kept in a barn that can still be seen from Lakeview Avenue. The building is a private residence today.

THE BLUFFS. Around 1910, Grosse Pointe was still a popular summer destination for wealthy families from Detroit. Summer cottages like Weeanne and Summerside dotted the bluff high about the shoreline. Soon the affluent families wanted permanent residences on the lake. The cottages were torn down, and opulent estates were built. Today luxury homes on Lake Shore Road and the subdivisions behind them replaced the estates that once ran from the lake up to present-day Mack Avenue.

ST. PAUL'S CEMETERY. A visit to St. Paul's Cemetery, located at the corner of Country Club Lane and Moross Road, is like a hands-on history lesson. Moved to this location in the late 1800s from the church property on the lake, the cemetery is the final resting place for many prominent Grosse Pointers, including members of the Moross, Allard, Cadieux, Beaufait, Moran, Trombley, Van Antwerp, Champine, and Neff families. The oldest grave, which was removed from the original cemetery, is that of Catherine Vernier, who died in 1831.

Provencal-Weir House. Believed to be the community's oldest surviving residence, this c. 1823 Greek Revival farmhouse was built by Detroiter Pierre Provencal on a site near Provencal and Lake Shore Roads. His daughter, Catherine, and her husband, Judge James D. Weir, used it for a summer cottage. Around 1914, it was moved to its present Kercheval Avenue location by John Labelle, who added the kitchen, dining room, and second-floor bedrooms. The Grosse Pointe Historical Society later purchased the house and in 1993 began an active restoration. Today the society holds regular events there that explore and celebrate many different aspects of Grosse Pointe history.

JOHN WYNNE JR. HOUSE ON LAKE SHORE ROAD. This charming, Victorian Queen Anne–style summer house was built around 1896 for John Wynne, a Detroit attorney. Wynne got the land on the lakeshore from his client Theodore P. Hall, whose summer home, Tonnancour, was nearby. The home is one of the last remaining of the Grosse Pointe summer cottages and is used as a residence today. Over the many generations, countless children and grandchildren have played games on the long front lawn that stretched to the lake when it was built and now ends at Lake Shore Road.

EDSEL AND ELEANOR FORD HOUSE. In 1926, Edsel and Eleanor Ford asked celebrated Detroit architect Albert Kahn to design a sprawling Cotswold-style estate on 21 parcels of land at Gaukler Point on Lake St. Clair. The couple raised their four children in the 60-room house surrounded by meadows and woods. After Edsel's death, Eleanor sold 44 acres of the property for $60,000 to Grosse Pointe Woods to develop its city park. The estate opened to the public in 1978 in accordance with provisions in her estate that it not be demolished. Since then, hundreds of thousands of visitors have toured the beautiful home, viewed the art and antiques collection, strolled the lovely grounds along the lake, and attended classes, lectures, and special events.

MILK RIVER. The Milk River, named for its cloudy, whitish-brown color, was once an important travel route for Native American and French settlers seeking an alternative when the waters of Lake St. Clair were too rough. A 1702 map of Lac Sainte Claire shows an Ottawa village near the Milk River. As early as 1796, some 30 French families had settled there. Both groups fished and hunted muskrat, catfish, and turtles in its waters. In 1974, the Milk River was partially covered up by the Wayne County Drain Commission and is now a storm drain. It also forms the waterway to the lake for the Grosse Pointe Woods park, and it is open where it passes under Lake Shore Road and alongside 10 houses inland.

CHAPTER 2

PREPARING FOR
HARVARD AND
HEAVEN

MAIRE ELEMENTARY SCHOOL. The Grosse Pointe Public School System as it is known was created in 1921. Previously five separate districts had served the children of the community. Over the two decades following its creation, surveys were conducted to determine future building and site needs and a flurry of new construction ensued. Maire Elementary School was completed in 1936 and named for Dr. Lewis Maire, a school board member who worked on the consolidation. The original grounds included tennis courts where the Kroger parking lot is today. The board of education sold the property along Kercheval Avenue in 1939 to make way for stores of the Village shopping district.

COOK SCHOOLHOUSE. The Cook Schoolhouse was built in 1890 on a third of an acre of the ribbon farm of Mathilda and Louis Cook, located near Mack Avenue and Renaud Street. Teachers received $1.50 per day and a one-year's supply of chalk and ink (which cost $1). Members of many of Grosse Pointe's founding families sent their children to the one-room schoolhouse, including the Cooks, Beaufaits, Trombleys, Van Antwerps, and Bryses. It was used as a school until 1922, then served as a church, music studio, apartment, and office. It was spared from demolition in 2006 when the owner donated the building to the City of Grosse Pointe Woods. It has been moved to Ghesquiere Park, and plans are to use it for community events and historic programs.

PREPARING FOR HARVARD AND HEAVEN

DEFER ELEMENTARY SCHOOL. The first school to be built after the consolidation of the Grosse Pointe Public School System was Defer Elementary School. It was constructed in 1925 on a former rhubarb patch on Ludwig Meininger's farm, which also included a strawberry field, an apple orchard, and dairy cows. Defer is the oldest school building still in use as a school today in Grosse Pointe and originally housed kindergarten through eighth grade. The first principal was Frederick Kerby, whose ancestors were among the first English settlers in the Pointes. The school has grown and adapted to the times, becoming the site of one of the district's first all-day kindergartens in 1985 and the district's first magnet program for gifted students in 1995. An elevator and air-conditioning have been added in recent years.

POUPARD ELEMENTARY SCHOOL. The only Grosse Pointe public school not located in Grosse Pointe, Poupard Elementary School opened at the corner of Van Antwerp and Harper Streets in Harper Woods in 1951 with 270 students. Four years later it had almost doubled in size and an additional gymnasium and classrooms were added to cope with the growing student population. At one time, it had as many as 850 students, but today enrollment is back down to its original size. It was named for Charles Poupard, treasurer of the board of education. His ancestors, Simon and Genevieve Beaubien Poupard (below), raised their family on a farm, purchased in 1860, which spanned most of Yorkshire Road in Grosse Pointe Park. The Poupards were active civic leaders, as were their descendants.

PREPARING FOR HARVARD AND HEAVEN

PIERCE MIDDLE SCHOOL. Completed in 1939, the John D. Pierce Junior High was the district's first junior high school. It was named after the state's first superintendent of schools and contained some high-tech elements for its day: a public address system, one-way glass, visual aids, and voice recording equipment. The main branch of the Grosse Pointe Public Library was originally housed in a wing of the school. Built to house 900 students in grades 7 through 9, today students in grades 7 through 8 attend the school. New, state-of-the-art science rooms have recently been completed.

GROSSE POINTE NORTH HIGH SCHOOL.
By the mid-1960s, the population surge in the Pointes had its only high school bursting at the seams and voters approved the building of a new high school. The board of education purchased the 31.7-acre Vanderbush Farm, the sole remaining such parcel in Grosse Pointe Woods and one of the last working farms in the Pointes. Grosse Pointe North High School opened in 1968. The structure was state of the art and included an academic building flanked on one side by large physical educational facilities and on the other side by an auditorium and music instruction rooms. Today it is home to more than 1,500 students in grades 9 through 12. Its refurbished performing arts center is used by all the schools in the district as well as other community groups.

PREPARING FOR HARVARD AND HEAVEN

"Then Conquer We Must, When Our Cause It Is Just"
—*The Star Spangled Banner*

We're doing our best, Mr. President.

Pearl Harbor found us already active in the war effort. Red Cross work, defense stamp sales, conservation such activities we had been stressing with increasing determination. Since December 7 we've doubled that determination, and we'll do it again.

Our country's entrance into the War of Survival brought us many new concerns. We had to begin thinking about protection in case of air raids, about first aid, about civilian defense. And now, more than ever we had to continue to do our share in the buying of war stamps and bonds.

Ten student-faculty committees are on the job to see to it that no precaution and no opportunity is overlooked.

We've knitted sweaters, made sandwiches, contributed books and magazines, painted menus, marched in parades, saved tin foil and paper and metal, walked to save tires, cut down on candy and cakes, pasted scrapbooks, studied maps — we've thought deep and hard.

Yes, Mr. President, we're doing our best ... but we know it's only a little compared to the great thing we may have to do.

GROSSE POINTE HIGH AIR RAID PRACTICE.

Grosse Pointe High School was not immune to the impact of World War II. A page in the 1942 school yearbook proclaims, "We're doing our best, Mr. President." Students knit sweaters, saved tin foil, and practiced air raid drills. Many seniors prepared to go into the service right after graduation. Today the students gather together for more upbeat purposes, as shown here during spirit week before homecoming.

GROSSE POINTE (SOUTH) HIGH SCHOOL. When plans to build a high school were proposed to Grosse Pointers in the early 1920s, quite a bit of opposition developed, even resulting in a lawsuit. Some believed they would never need a building so large and luxurious; others hoped the highly regarded Detroit system would take over. But in 1928, the Georgian-style building with its distinguished clock tower was completed. Architect George Haas was directed to "create in appearance an expression in brick and mortar of the idealism of the public school in community and individual life," according to the dedication program. The school has undergone numerous additions and modernizations, though all of the original building remains.

PREPARING FOR HARVARD AND HEAVEN

UNIVERSITY LIGGETT SCHOOL. Detroit University School, a boys day school formerly located near Detroit's Indian Village, moved to this new school building on Cook Road near Chalfonte in Grosse Pointe Woods in 1929, with the help of Edsel and Henry Ford, among others. In 1941, it merged administratively with Grosse Pointe Country Day School. The two schools became one, under the name Grosse Pointe University School, in 1953. A few years later, the Liggett School, a private girls academy, moved from Indian Village and merged with Grosse Pointe University School to create today's University Liggett School. The celebrated, modern architect Minoru Yamasaki designed the lower and middle school and headmaster's house.

VERNIER SCHOOL. Designed by Albert Kahn and built in 1916 on Vernier Road in Grosse Pointe Shores, the Vernier School had seven classrooms, including one with a pewabic tile fireplace decorated with figures of rabbits, ducks, roosters, and antelopes. It was used as a school until the early 1950s and then as storage for the shores municipal offices while they decided its fate. The city polled its citizens, and almost two-thirds responded that it should be demolished rather than spend the estimated $1.5–2 million to restore and maintain it. It was razed in 1994, and new houses and condominiums were built on the site. The school bell was saved and is located near the municipal building.

CADIEUX SCHOOL. In 1906, Grosse Pointe School District No. 1 built its second school building, a two-story brick structure at 389 St. Clair Avenue in the village of Grosse Pointe. Another building was constructed next door, and by 1924, the school housed all area students from kindergarten through grade 12. Cadieux School was so overcrowded that double sessions had to be scheduled. The congestion was alleviated when the high school opened in 1928. The district, whose offices have been located here since 1929, had planned to vacate the two buildings, but the decision was met with great public outcry and a bid to purchase the property was rejected. In 2002 and 2003, the buildings underwent a major renovation.

KERBY ELEMENTARY SCHOOL. By 1857, children of Grosse Pointe were studying reading, writing, and arithmetic in the original Kerby Elementary School, the first public school in Grosse Pointe. It was a one-room wooden structure situated on the Alexander Michie farm on Lake Shore Road between Moran and Kerby Roads. In 1886, Kerby students moved north to a clapboard structure on Kerby Road, at the present-day site of the Grosse Pointe Farms municipal offices. A brick building was constructed in 1905 to replace the old wooden schoolhouse. By 1949, an ever-growing enrollment forced the school to relocate to its present site on Kerby and Beaupre Roads in Grosse Pointe Farms.

TROMBLY ELEMENTARY SCHOOL. Trombly is another school that has had many buildings. The first one, built in 1861, was a frame school named District One (above). In 1903, the original Robert Trombly school was built on the corner of Jefferson and Beaconsfield Avenues. It was a fine school in its day with four large rooms for its 100 students, five teachers, and the principal, who also taught. On a clear day, the students could see the big ships passing along the shores of Lake St. Clair. By the early 1920s, the building was showing signs of wear and all the students were sent to Defer Elementary School, which had just been built. Very shortly, however, Defer began to get too crowded and the need for another Trombly School became apparent. The new school took only six months to erect. Designed by the firm of Smith, Hinchman and Grylls Associates, it opened in January 1927, at Beaconsfield and Essex Avenues.

GROSSE POINTE ACADEMY GROUNDS. Today's Grosse Pointe Academy was founded in 1885 as the all-girls Academy of the Sacred Heart by the nuns of the Religious of the Sacred Heart. The original property, a ribbon farm in design, ran from the lake to Ridge Road. Until the late 1940s, the property was a self-sustaining farm. Along Moran Road was a large chicken house. Toward Grosse Pointe Boulevard were apple, pear, and cherry trees, grape arbors, and some raspberry bushes. In the 1920s, the nuns sold the property from Grosse Pointe Boulevard to Ridge Road and used the money for a major building program that included construction of the present facility.

PREPARING FOR HARVARD AND HEAVEN

GROSSE POINTE ACADEMY. The first Catholic boarding school for girls, the Academy of the Sacred Heart, was built on a bluff very close to the water's edge in 1885. Three decades later, increasing enrollment prompted the construction of the academic building still used today, which was designed in a Tudor Revival style by the nationally prominent architects Schickel, Maginnis and Walsh. In 1969, the nuns deeded the school and all buildings to a lay board of trustees and the school became Grosse Pointe Academy, a coeducational, nondenominational school. A modern fieldhouse and performing arts facility were recently added, and a complete renovation of the main school is currently underway.

Convent of the Sacred Heart, Grosse Pointe Farms, Michigan. Early Spring

ST. PAUL ROMAN CATHOLIC CHURCH. The Gothic Revival, fieldstone and brick structure where a parish of some 2,500 families worships today is actually the third St. Paul church building. The first was a small log chapel with a dirt floor built in 1825 on part of the Renaud property near present-day Vernier Road and the lake. The growing congregation prompted the purchase of the present-day site on Lake Shore Road. A frame edifice of local timber was built in 1857 where sermons were in French until the 1880s. As the 20th century dawned, today's 640-seat church was constructed under the guidance of Fr. John Eisen, who never lived to see it occupied. In fact, his funeral was the first Mass celebrated in the new church.

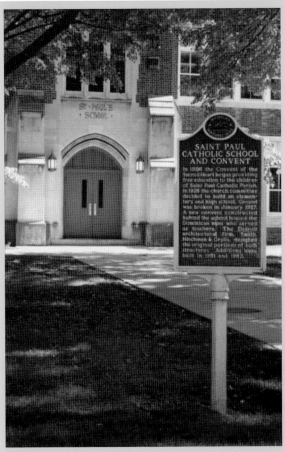

St. Paul School. In 1926, the St. Paul Parish decided to build its own school, after nearly 40 years of sending its children to a free school run by the Convent of the Sacred Heart next door. In 1951 and 1963, the gymnasium, 11 classrooms, and the cafeteria were constructed. In keeping with educational trends and needs of the community, a kindergarten program, preschool program, half-day young fives program, full-day kindergarten, and extended day care program have all been added. The building is on the National Register of Historic Places. In 2006, the school was designated a Blue Ribbon School for academic excellence by the U.S. Department of Education.

GROSSE POINTE MEMORIAL CHURCH.
Beginning with the early settlers in the 1750s, Grosse Pointers have been predominantly Catholic. But with the advent of summer residents, local Protestants found enough members to form the Grosse Pointe Protestant Evangelical Association. The "Little Ivy Covered Church" on Lake Shore Road near Fisher Road was their second church. Nondenominational at first, the congregation became Presbyterian and a new church, the present neo-Gothic structure, was built in 1927. Truman H. Newberry and his brother John funded the new sanctuary in honor of their parents, and the name was changed to the Grosse Pointe Memorial Church. A major renovation project was completed in 1997 that included a new lakeside entry and reception area, the creation of a sacristy, and the installation of an elevator.

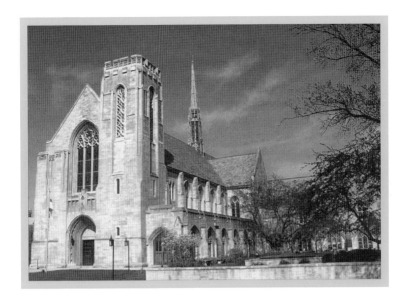

CHRIST CHURCH GROSSE POINTE. Begun as a 1923 mission of Christ Church Detroit, Christ Church Grosse Pointe dedicated a sanctuary in 1930. The elegant neo-Gothic structure was designed by Bertram G. Goodhues Associates, the New York firm that also created the magnificent Christ Church Cranbrook in Bloomfield Hills. The church was built like those of the Middle Ages using wooden pegs instead of nails, and stone and mortar instead of plaster. Because the church was one of the few built during the Depression, many outstanding artisans were available to beautify it with intricate wood carving and detailed stonework. In 2000, a 32,000-square-foot Christian education wing and five new stained-glass windows were completed.

CHRIST CHURCH, GROSSE POINTE, MICHIGAN

ST. AMBROSE CATHOLIC CHURCH. St. Ambrose parish was established in 1916 by Bishop John Foley and first worshiped from a frame church in Grosse Pointe Park. The current structure, a beautiful Norman Gothic church designed by architects Donaldson and Meier, opened on Christmas Eve in 1927. It was lauded in *American Architecture Magazine* for its attention to detail and use of the latest technology. A grade school opened in 1920 with 650 students; later a high school was added. Both are closed now, but the parish continues to be active in education and community outreach. In 2002, the ARK, an innovative, underground gathering place, was built. Designed by Latvian-born architect Gunnar Birkets with expansive skylights through which the facade of the historic church can be seen, the activity center is an exciting symbol of the rebirth of the parish.

How to Succeed in Business

MULIER'S MARKET. The first Mulier's Market was opened by Belgian immigrant Valere Mulier around 1917 near Mack Avenue and Woodhall Street in Detroit. His son Omer moved the store to Kercheval Avenue in Grosse Pointe Park in the late 1930s. The sawdust-covered wood floors remain today, as does the great customer service and personal attention. The store is still on Kercheval Avenue and is owned by Valere's great-grandson Mike Mulier.

THE OLD PLACE. It was known as a unique restaurant for special occasions, but older patrons could tell tales of its more colorful origins and intriguing owner. Al Green was a native Chicagoan who came to Detroit in 1921 at the tender age of 19 and quickly became a successful bootlegger. He and his wife, Torchie, ran Grosse Pointe's most famous speakeasy, the Pines, at Lothrop Road near Ridge Road, where blue blood mixed with blue collar to enjoy Green's special spirits. After Prohibition ended, Green became a respectable citizen, running a successful catering business and two restaurants, Al Green's on the Hill and the Al Green Restaurant, later the Old Place. It was razed, and new condominiums stand there today.

ESQUIRE THEATRE. The Esquire Theatre, a large art deco–style neighborhood house was built in 1938 on Jefferson Avenue near Nottingham Street. With seating around 1,000, the Esquire served as a first-run theater for much of the time it operated until it was acquired by P and R Theater Company in 1980 and switched to second-run features. P and R also installed 14 video games in the lobby, inciting city leaders. Causing another bit of controversy in 1982, P and R screened the notorious adult film *Debbie Does Dallas*. New owners, Eric and Ervin Steiner, divided the house into four small auditoriums, returning to first-run films in 1983. In 1988, the city closed the Esquire. It was demolished in 1990 and is now a parking lot for condominiums.

JOHN BERY'S MEAT MARKET. This market, which opened in the mid-1890s, was located at Maryland Street and Jefferson Avenue in Grosse Pointe Park, though the property extended to Fox Creek. A slaughterhouse and smokehouse occupied the back barn. Bert Bery and A. C. Butler drove a horse-drawn wagon from farm to farm in Grosse Pointe for fresh livestock. The meat hung by the hoof, and Bery and Butler cut it to order. The Bery family lived on the property. Son George Bery was still a butcher into the 1980s, first at Henri's in the Village and later at Hamlin's. Both of these stores are also gone. The original site of Bery's market is now where the Grosse Pointe Park municipal building stands.

BON SECOURS HOSPITAL. In 1909, five Sisters of Bon Secours arrived in Michigan from Baltimore, embarking on a mission of nursing the sick and indigent in their homes. In 1924, the sisters purchased a farmhouse and four-acre lot in Grosse Pointe that later became an eight-bed convalescent home. In January 1945, Bon Secours Hospital opened as a true 36-bed facility. New wings were added in the 1950s, a parking deck was built in 1971, and a $30 million expansion and modernization project was completed in 1980. Today the hospital has 290 licensed beds. It merged with Cottage Hospital and is currently up for sale.

THE VILLAGE. This corner of Notre Dame Street and Kercheval Avenue was originally occupied by the Grosse Pointe Shop operated by John and Augusta Verfaille. Built in the 1920s, it was one of the first commercial buildings on the street. The shopping district, known as the Village, has been providing customers with a personal touch since then. Built on the "back forty" of farmland granted to Robert and James Abbott, the first stores were located in clapboard homes scattered along old Kercheval Avenue, originally called Field Street. Today many national chains have replaced some of the local shops. At this site today is a very popular Starbucks coffee shop.

HOW TO SUCCEED IN BUSINESS

THE GROSSE POINTE SHOP. The dry goods store known as the Grosse Pointe Shop sold clothing, shoes, and accessories to Grosse Pointers in this typical storefront in the Village. It was relatively small by today's standards at only about 20 feet wide by 40 feet deep. Proprieter Augusta Verfaille and her daughter Stella, shown here, lived in one of the three apartments upstairs until the 1960s. Augusta's father, Henry Huvaere, added adjoining buildings to the original store, which were occupied by the Village's first Kroger grocery store and Russell Piche's barbershop. Posterity, a gallery, shown here, occupies the building now (notice the same support pole), along with franchises of national chains and some local specialty stores.

NOTRE DAME PHARMACY TO COLDWATER CREEK. The original Notre Dame Pharmacy was built in the 1920s by pharmacist Fred Knuff on Kercheval Avenue and Notre Dame Street, across the street from the Grosse Pointe Shop in the 1920s. Employees went to great lengths to keep their customers happy. Once a woman calling in an order added that she had lost her dog and asked if the delivery man would mind calling for Goofy on his walk over to make the delivery. He cheerfully complied. From the 1940s through 2002, the corner was the location of the Village's legendary anchor store, Jacobson's. Today the site is occupied by Coldwater Creek, a women's clothing chain.

JACOBSON'S. The flagship retail establishment of the Village for many generations of shoppers was Jacobson's department store. It opened in Grosse Pointe as a women's store in 1944 on Kercheval Avenue. It later added a men's department, children's department, a full line of gifts and accessories, and a home furnishings store in a separate building down the street. The main store had a restaurant, the St. Clair Room. The store grew with the economy, adding 35,000 square feet of selling space in the early 1970s, but by 2002, the venerable store had declared bankruptcy and closed. Today the space is occupied by JoS. A. Banks and Coldwater Creek. A Trader Joe's is expected to join them.

SANDERS. When Fred Sanders opened a Grosse Pointe store in 1934, the magnificent hot fudge cream puffs were only 15¢ and a scoop of ice cream cost a dime. This location was a local lunch hangout in the Village for decades, offering a variety of sandwiches and soups. Throughout most of the 1960s until the store closed in the late 1990s, many of its employees were fixtures in the community, having worked there for 35–40 years. The space is still a favorite meeting place and today is occupied by Caribou Coffee.

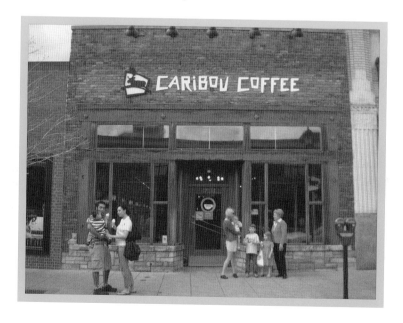

HOW TO SUCCEED IN BUSINESS

HICKEY'S WALTON PIERCE. In 1947, Henrietta Warnick Pierce moved her well-respected couturier, Walton Pierce, from the Women's City Club on Park Avenue in Detroit to the Village, ushering in an elegant level of personal service that defined a shopping era. Customers included the upper crust of the community such as Edsel Ford's wife, Eleanor; even Mrs. J. L. Hudson had clothes custom made there. Walton Pierce is located at this corner of Kercheval Avenue and St. Clair Avenue, sharing the store with venerable men's clothier E. J. Hickey's, a partner since 1997. Another of downtown Detroit's finest establishments, E. J. Hickey's came to the Village in the 1950s. Pierce's grandson Bill Huntington and his wife, Mary Jo, own the store, which still prides itself on old-fashioned commitment and service to its customers.

MACK 7 DINER. Piche and Dunning's Refreshments, near the corner of Mack Avenue and Moross Road (Seven Mile Road), has been a popular hangout since it opened in the 1920s. Its famous hot dogs were made even more delectable by its homemade mustard relish. The restaurant is still owned by the same family after four generations. Today the Mack 7 Diner serves short-order breakfast and lunch to hungry Grosse Pointe area residents, workers, and descendants of the original customers.

SCHETTLER'S. This location on Jefferson Avenue has served the needs of local residents in a wide variety of ways since before World War I. The original building was wooden, built by a Dr. Belanger who lived upstairs and ran a drugstore downstairs in the early 1900s. Schettler Drugs moved into the building around 1918. There was a soda fountain in the store as well as a pharmacy. The western side of the building was occupied by Nagle's hardware store at one time. Schettler Drugs merged with Cunningham Drug Stores in the 1940s, but Schettler's finally closed in 1947. The Grosse Pointe Bank moved in after that. National Bank of Detroit purchased the building in 1954. Since then, the bank has changed hands a number of times. The current resident is Chase Bank.

FARMS POLICE. Grosse Pointe Farms' finest enjoy their new village hall, built on Kerby Road after an old frame Protestant church was moved to this location in 1894 to serve as the village hall. Less than 20 years later, they had a new home on the current site, Kerby Road just past Grosse Pointe Boulevard. This 1912 structure (above), designed by Mildner and Eisen, had room for a seven-member combined police and fire department. On the left side of the building is the old Kerby School. The building has been remodeled and enlarged several times since then; the last time was in the late 1980s.

PUNCH AND JUDY THEATRE. With a design by Robert O. Derrick and financial backing by such Grosse Pointe VIPs as Edsel Ford, Roy Chapin, Wendell Anderson, and Lawrence Buhl, it is no wonder the Punch and Judy Theatre building opened with much fanfare in 1930. Moviegoers watched classics like *The Maltese Falcon* and *Bringing Up Baby* for 10¢ (12¢ in the loge) in the 1930s and 1940s. In the late 1970s, it changed to a repertory house most noted for showing *The Rocky Horror Picture Show*. New wave and punk rock bands like Talking Heads, Devo, B-52s, the Clash, and the Ramones shocked Grosse Pointe with performances there in the 1970s and 1980s. None of these could make the theater profitable enough, and in 1987, it became a commercial office building.

PONGRACZ JEWELERS. Located on Kercheval Avenue on the Hill today, Pongracz's original store opened on Kercheval Avenue in the Village in the 1920s. Jeweler Ed Pongracz opened a watch and jewelry repair bench at the front of his father's interior decorator studio next to Jayne's Hardware. Pongracz moved his store to the Hill after World War II. He also built the adjoining building and offices above. It was sold recently and is now called Pongracz-LaLonde Jewelers and Gemologists. It is still one of the finest and most well-respected jewelers in Grosse Pointe today.

THE HILL. As Grosse Pointe's residential areas expanded, so did its shopping districts. In the late 1920s, a new commercial center was created that became known as the Hill. The Punch and Judy Theatre building was one of its first commercial buildings, opening in 1930. With it, the block took on the character of 18th-century Boston or a provincial English town. By 1940, the business district extended from Fisher Road (shown here) to Muir Road, the site of Cottage Hospital. William Denler's Interior Design Studio, Paselk Florist, and the Sign of the Mermaid were among the first shops there.

COTTAGE HOSPITAL. When the great Spanish influenza swept Grosse Pointe in 1918, a number of prominent women in the community—the Baroness Maud Ledyard Von Kettler, Anna Dodge, and Ethel DuPont Roosevelt Warren among them—rallied to create a hospital to care for the sick of the area. A small cottage on Oak Street (now Muir Road) was purchased and renovated in 1919. It became the first Cottage Hospital with five adult beds, five children's beds, and three bassinets. Within months, demand increased and the house next door was purchased and an operating suite and maternity unit were built. The current facility opened in 1928 at its present site on Kercheval Avenue. The hospital has since merged with Bon Secours Hospital and is currently up for sale.

GROSSE POINTE SHORES MUNICIPAL BUILDING AND VILLAGE HALL. This Federal-style building with arched windows and intricate brickwork was designed by Albert Kahn in 1915 on property purchased from Henry Ford for the Grosse Pointe Shores Village Hall and municipal building. Located on Vernier Road and Lake Shore Road, it is an excellent example of how Kahn could use brick masonry in a decorative way. In 1984, renovations included a glass stairwell and an elevator. Next to the building, which is still in use today, is a new athletic field called Ford Park, a sledding hill, a baseball diamond, and a dog park.

WOODS THEATER. The Woods Theater on Mack Avenue in Grosse Pointe Woods was a house of dreams for generations of Grosse Pointers for more than 40 years. The movie house was bought by AMC Theatres in the 1980s. The company closed it in 1997, claiming the six-screen theater could not compete with the megaplexes with 20 or more screens. At the time, it was the only remaining movie theater in the five Grosse Pointes. St. John Hospital purchased the property for about $2.5 million.

GROSSE POINTE WOODS POLICE STATION. Grosse Pointe Woods municipal workers, police officers, and firefighters were delighted to move into the new municipal building on Mack Avenue between Torrey and Kenmore Roads in 1963. Behind the building is Ghesquiere Park and its baseball diamonds, soccer fields, playscapes, and hockey rink. The sprawling facility was a significant upgrade to the old building on Anita Road and Mack Avenue, where a municipal parking lot now stands. In 1990, a community center was added to the municipal building. Activities ranging from senior citizen luncheons to preschool dance classes bring in many residents everyday.

HOWARD JOHNSON'S RESTAURANT. The restaurant, with its famous orange tile roof, occupied the property where the CVS Pharmacy now stands on Mack Avenue in Grosse Pointe Woods. Locals dined on its famous fried clams, burgers, and ice-cream sundaes for decades. Later a Red Lobster occupied the building briefly. Then a drugstore chain, now CVS, built on the site and is still there today.

CHAPTER 4

PLAY IT AGAIN, OLD SPORT

HORSE AND BUGGY. Out for an afternoon ride, these young ladies pose before trotting on their way. The panorama was lovely, and the gentle wind off the lake was a delight at the edge of the late-19th-century Tonnancour estate of Theodore Parsons Hall, near today's Tonnancour Place and Lake Shore Road. Their counterparts today might stop at the same spot to catch a breeze or take in the view of the water or lakefront houses. Though much has changed from the days of Tonnancour, the scene is just as beautiful.

SS *Delphine II*. Automobile mogul Horace Dodge was as much a fan of boating as he was of cars. He had built a succession of luxury yachts when he commissioned the SS *Delphine II* in 1920. After Dodge's untimely death, his wife, Anna, oversaw the yacht's completion at a cost of $2 million. In true entrepreneurial spirit, the SS *Delphine II* has reinvented herself as often as needed to survive. She was totally rebuilt after catching fire and sinking in 1926. She was acquired by the U.S. Navy during World War II to be used in training missions, then changed hands numerous times until being sold to the current owner in 1997. The yacht has been restored to her original splendor and was rechristened in 2003 by Princess Stephanie of Monaco, where she is currently docked.

SS _Delphine II_ Interior. Launched in April 1921, four months after Horace Dodge's death, the 258-foot steam yacht SS _Delphine II_, had a power system designed by Dodge himself. Named for Dodge's only daughter, the yacht had five decks, a 25-by-20-foot owner's stateroom, and nine guest staterooms with private connecting baths. The main deck contained a music room with a $60,000 pipe organ. Aft of the music room was a passenger lounge inlaid entirely in teak. The yacht has been completely refurbished by the owner, a Belgian textile tycoon, and is available for chartered trips in the western Mediterranean for a mere 50,000 euros per day (about $67,000) in the high season. Of course, this does not include a "hairdresser; massage person; fitness person; bodyguards and musicians," according to the yacht's official Web site.

SAILING. Life on the water has always been a chief attraction of Grosse Pointe, as these 1930s sailors (above) would have attested. Lake St. Clair's appeal has attracted pleasure crafts and racing vessels to its sparkling waters for decades. On any given summer afternoon, the lake is the site of sailing lessons taking place just off the yacht clubs' docks. As evening approaches, landlubbers can see the colorful billowing sails of weekday regattas that are sponsored by the municipal parks and private clubs.

NEIGHBORHOOD CLUB. The first meeting of the Grosse Pointe Neighborhood Club was held in 1911 when a board of 24 women, mostly summer residents, elected Marion J. Alger as president. Their goal was to provide recreation and social services to the area's residents, focusing on employees of the great estates and their families. The Neighborhood Club cosponsored Grosse Pointe's first public library in 1915 and helped organize Grosse Pointe's first hospital in 1917. In 1927, the building shown below was constructed on an eight-acre site donated by Dexter M. Ferry Jr. The club continued to expand its offerings and in 1968 built its current facility, a 13,500-square-foot center directly across the street on Waterloo Road and St. Clair Avenue.

WAR MEMORIAL GARDENS. When New York architect Charles Platt was designing the Moorings estate for Russell A. Alger Jr. around 1910, he called on landscape architect Ellen Biddle Shipman, his frequent collaborator, to design its formal gardens. Beyond the pergola was a lawn stretching down to the lake. In 1962, the Fries Auditorium and Crystal Ballroom were built on that lawn. The front part of the gardens remain with a reflecting pool for the enjoyment of all who visit the site, which is now known as the Grosse Pointe War Memorial, a community center.

Farms Pier
1941

PIER PARK. In 1909, residents of Grosse Pointe Farms petitioned for the establishment of a public park. A few years later, the city purchased the property at Moross and Lake Shore Roads for that purpose. A convenience station and the pier for which the park is named were built by the early 1920s. Since then, countless children have had fun in the waves diving off the pier or wading in from the beach. A pool was later built, but park-goers still enjoy taking a dip in the lake, an exclusive privilege of Grosse Pointe Farms residents whose park is the only one with swimming access to Lake St. Clair.

GROSSE POINTE LIBRARY SYSTEM.
Today's library system has come a long way since its first stand-alone home—a cottage next to the Neighborhood Club on Waterloo Avenue donated by Dexter M. Ferry Jr. in 1926. Three branches comprising 61,000 square feet of space now serve the Pointes. The central branch was designed by internationally acclaimed architect Marcel Breuer in 1953. Two new libraries were recently built, replacing older, smaller branches: the Ewald branch in Grosse Pointe Park in 2004 and the Woods branch in 2006, shown here. Both offer state-of-the-art technology, story time rooms, teen areas, study rooms, and comfortable seating. Between the three branches, the library system has about 170,000 books and 33,000 videos, DVDs, CDs, and other items to lend and regularly features guest lecturers and other special programs.

PIER PARK BOATHOUSE. In the 1960s, Grosse Pointe Farms residents had it pretty good with their modern community building that served as a warming station for skaters in the winter (below). The small harbor behind the building made a perfect rink that was sheltered somewhat from the vast lake beyond. Today the harbor is a bit more crowded after a major renovation of the park in 2006 added much-needed new boat slips and docks. A new community center (above) was the showpiece of the renovation. It rivals any social club with a stylish lobby, two beautiful reception rooms, a granite and stainless steel kitchen, and a wrap-around porch that overlooks the harbor and lake. Life is good.

GAZEBO. Legend has it that this 1893 lakeside shrine on the Tonnancour estate was the site where Genevieve Parent, known as the Nun of St. Clair, hid to escape the unrelenting advances of a suitor who had been transformed into a wolf. The story goes that the wolf, La Loup Garou, was turned into stone as he leapt toward her on the rocks and his evil face can still be seen, frozen in granite, on the beach there near the foot of Tonnancour Road. Today very near that spot is the gazebo (above) at Pier Park where much calmer courtships take place.

HUNT CLUB. Originally known as the Grosse Pointe Country Club, the Hunt Club was founded in 1911, the heyday of polo and foxhunting, by a group of Detroit's most esteemed horsemen, including the Algers, Dodges, Fishers, Fords, and Whitneys. The club had been an institution on Cook Road when tragedy struck in 2001. A fire set by a recklessly tossed firecracker destroyed the club's nearly 100-year-old barn, killing 19 horses. The devastated members vowed not to let the catastrophe bring down their beloved club, and a new barn was built soon after.

FISHING RODEO. "Are they biting?" is a question asked from early spring to late autumn in Grosse Pointe as Lake St. Clair draws fishermen of all ages and abilities to cast for walleye, perch, and smallmouth bass. A great tradition going back more than 50 years in the municipal parks is the fishing rodeo, where kids from all ages compete for prizes and the thrill of trying to land "the big one" (or maybe it is just the free hot dog lunch they are after). In the c. 1950 picture above, a proud contestant displays his award. Everyone is a winner in the rodeos today (below) and the prizes take the sting out of a fruitless day at sea.

WOODS PARK SWIMMING. Though not the pristine Olympic-sized pool in use today, this swimming hole at the Grosse Pointe Woods Lake Front Park did the trick in the 1950s. Built using a cofferdam at the mouth of the Milk River, it was sealed off from Lake St. Clair and used filtered lake water. The round pool was 100 yards in diameter, and at the time it was the largest municipal swimming pool in the country. In 1976, Woods residents approved a $2 million bond proposal to build a new swimming pool in the park, along with a bathhouse, tennis courts, and parking lots. The former cofferdam was covered with dirt and grass and is now an open area along the lakeshore. A 31-foot-high waterslide was added in 1997 to the squealing delight of the children of Grosse Pointe Woods.

FOURTH OF JULY. Grosse Pointe has always been a patriotic community, and the Fourth of July has been a cause for great celebration over the years. In the picture below, the George B. Russel family commemorates Independence Day in 1891 with a family gathering at their summer home, Rest Cottage, which stood on Lake Shore Road near Moran Road. More than 100 years later, the holiday is just as important, as this group of modern patriots enjoys a picnic at the park followed by fireworks over the lake.

A Fourth of July party about 1891.

SKATING. Boating and fishing are not the only ways Grosse Pointers have enjoyed Lake St. Clair over the years. Today's winter sports enthusiasts may not believe it, but in the 1800s and 1900s, the lake would freeze from shore to shore during normal winters. These Academy of the Sacred Heart students get their winter exercise on the frozen lake in front of their school in the late 1800s. Today's kids enjoy hockey and figure skating whenever they can, here at a Winterfest celebration on the lake.

VERNIER ROADHOUSE. John Vernier opened a roadhouse along the shore of his 400-acre farm at today's Vernier Road and Lake Shore Road in 1888. The eatery catered to travelers along the lake and adventurous Detroiters enjoying a day in the country and Vernier's famous chicken, fish, and frog leg dinners. He sold the roadhouse in 1895 to his cousin Edmund Vernier, who moved the business inland. Edmund was known for his hospitality, and the inn was one of the area's most popular during the Gay Nineties. In 1915, the business was moved again, making room for the Grosse Pointe Yacht Club. The club's gatehouse, shown here, is situated very close to the site of the original roadhouse.

GROSSE POINTE YACHT CLUB. The club was founded in 1914, though the clubhouse was not built until 1929. Iceboating was as popular as sailing then, and early records of the club list prizes including a lumberman's shirt and buckskin mittens awarded to iceboat race winners. In 1926, Rear Commodore C. L. Ayers personally purchased the property at Vernier and Lake Shore Roads. Guy Lowell designed the magnificent club based on Venetian motifs, with the campanile rising 187 feet above Lake St. Clair. It remains a navigational landmark for boaters. The club facilities have been updated and modernized several times. The harbor has been enlarged and improved as membership has quadrupled.

COUNTRY CLUB OF DETROIT. The first Country Club of Detroit golf course was situated on three miles of leased land along the shoreline of Lake St. Clair. Soon the club began looking for land it could own outright and purchased the Provencal-Weir Farm along the northeast edge of Grosse Pointe Farms, its current location. Famous British golf course designer H. S. Colt was hired to create the course, which included a polo field at the edge of the fairway. Albert Kahn was again commissioned, and his second clubhouse was finished in 1923. That structure burned to the ground two years later. Club members immediately began thinking about a new clubhouse and secured the firm of Smith, Hinchman and Grylls. Their rambling Tudor-style clubhouse opened in 1927 and is still in use today.

THE GROSSE POINTE CLUB. By the mid-1880s, the center of social life for most of Grosse Pointe's well-heeled summer residents was the Grosse Pointe Club. Its elaborate clubhouse and seven acres of land on the lake near Fisher Road allowed members to socialize, entertain, and participate in sports like lawn tennis, sailing, and golf. The club only lasted a few years, however, possibly due to its relatively remote location. It reopened as a casino, and in 1897, was leased by the newly formed Country Club of Detroit as its first clubhouse. Today a few luxury lakefront homes sit on its former property.

THE LITTLE CLUB. In 1923, the Grosse Pointe Club reopened near its original site. Prior to the construction of this clubhouse, which was built in 1927, a residence next to the club's property served as the clubhouse. Mainly a social club today, from the late 1920s to late 1940s, members participated in competitive sailing. The atmosphere of the club, more commonly known as the Little Club, has always been understated and close-knit. It is still considered one of the most prestigious and exclusive in the area. This building still serves as the clubhouse today.

DISCOVER THOUSANDS OF LOCAL HISTORY BOOKS FEATURING MILLIONS OF VINTAGE IMAGES

Arcadia Publishing, the leading local history publisher in the United States, is committed to making history accessible and meaningful through publishing books that celebrate and preserve the heritage of America's people and places.

Find more books like this at
www.arcadiapublishing.com

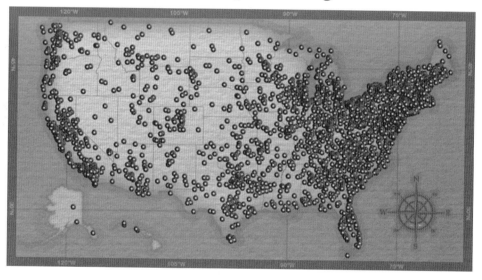

Search for your hometown history, your old stomping grounds, and even your favorite sports team.

COME FLY WITH ME. Though Russell A. Alger Jr., was chiefly known for his work directing the Packard Motor Company, he was also quite intrigued by the possibilities of the flying business. He went to France to watch the Wright Brother's exhibition and was so impressed that he invested money in their first commercial airplane. As a gift, they gave him this No. 6 biplane in 1911. Here it is waiting for takeoff from the former site of the Country Club of Detroit golf club. Such a trip in the same location would not be possible today—it is the present site of the Grosse Pointe South High School athletic field on Fisher Road.